FOOTBALL
MATH ON THE GRIDIRON

↑ BY TOM ROBINSON

Published by The Child's World®
1980 Lookout Drive • Mankato, MN 56003-1705
800-599-READ • www.childsworld.com

Acknowledgments
The Child's World®: Mary Berendes, Publishing Director
The Design Lab: Design and production
Red Line Editorial: Editorial direction

Photographs ©: Richard Paul Kane/Shutterstock Images,
Cover, Title; Paul Spinelli/AP Images, 4, 26; Shutterstock
Images, 6–7; Bill Nichols/Shutterstock, 9; Evan Pinkus/
AP Images, 10; Aspen Photo/Shutterstock Images, 12,
14–15, 23; David Stluka/AP Images, 17; Walter G Arce/
Shutterstock Images, 19; David Drapkin/AP Images, 21,
29; Carlos E. Santa Maria/Shutterstock Images, 24–25

ISBN 9781614734093
LCCN 2012946504

Printed in the United States of America
Mankato, MN
November, 2012
PA02144

ABOUT THE AUTHOR

Tom Robinson is the author of 33 books, including 25 about sports. The Susquehanna, Pennsylvania, native is an award-winning sportswriter and former newspaper sports editor.

TABLE OF CONTENTS

MATH ON THE GRIDIRON 4

THE BASICS 6

The Field	6
Managing the Game	8
Scoring Points	10
Conversions	12

THE PLAYERS 14

Big, Fast Guys	14
Comparing Statistics	16
Rating the Passers	18

THE TEAM 20

Filling the Roster	20
Turnover Differential	22
Covering Space	24
Two-Minute Drill	26

GO FIGURE 28
GLOSSARY 30
LEARN MORE 31
INDEX 32

New England
Patriots coach
Bill Belichick
yells toward the
field during a
game against
the Buffalo Bills
on November 18,
2007.

MATH ON THE GRIDIRON

Tom Brady completes a 5-yard pass on **first down**. New England Patriots coach Bill Belichick considers the next play. Belichick knows the team needs 5 more yards for a first down. In most games, football teams start out with four downs to make 10 yards. After gaining 5 yards, there are 5 yards left.

Two more yards are gained on a second down. Now, the Patriots need 3 yards for a new set of downs. Belichick considers his options. He also quickly uses simple math. How many yards are left? That question is a big part of the plays he calls.

$$\begin{array}{r} 10 \text{ YARDS} \\ - \ 5 \text{ YARDS} \\ \hline 5 \text{ YARDS} \end{array}$$

Football coaches know how to add to the yard-line number when figuring the length of a **field goal**. Math helps a coach do his job. It also helps fans follow football. Use your math skills as you take a look at football. You'll be surprised at how much they are needed!

THE BASICS

The Field

Football has one of the largest fields in sports. The field has markings, called hash marks. They show each single yard. Thicker lines show every 5 yards. The field also has border lines on all sides. Goal lines are near each end of the field. Teams score touchdowns by crossing the goal line into the **end zone**.

A football field is 120 yards long. It measures 100 yards from one goal line to the other. Each end zone adds 10 more yards.

100 + 10 + 10 = 120 total yards in length

53 1/3 YARDS

100 YARDS

10 YARDS

The field is 53 1/3 yards wide, or 53 yards and 1 foot. We can use the width and length to find the perimeter and area of a football field. Perimeter is the distance around something. We find the perimeter by adding the lengths of the four sides. A football field is a rectangle. A rectangle is a four-sided figure. Its opposite sides are parallel and the same length.

Perimeter = (length x 2) + (width x 2)

The perimeter of the field in yards is:
120 x 2 = 240
53 1/3 x 2 = 106 2/3
240 + 106 2/3 = 346 2/3 yards

The perimeter of the field is
346 2/3 yards.

10 YARDS

Area is the amount of space inside a shape. A rectangle's area is found by multiplying length times width. To find this total as a whole number, use feet. First change the length and width to feet. There are 3 feet in 1 yard. Area is shown in square units.

Area = length x width

120 yards x 3 = 360 feet
(53 yards x 3) + 1 foot = 160 feet
360 feet x 160 feet = 57,600 square feet

The area of the field is 57,600 square feet.

7

Managing the Game

Football games are split into four quarters. The quarters are 15 minutes each for pro and college. They are 12 minutes each in high school. Youth games are shorter.

The clock stops at various times. Two examples are incomplete passes and plays that go out-of-bounds. While they try to score, teams keep the ball by advancing 10 yards in four plays or less for a first down. Repeated first downs allow a team to have possession, or hold the ball longer. With longer possessions, a team gets more plays to score. This also limits the plays by the opposite team. Total time of possession is a **statistic** used to compare teams in a game.

The New York Giants defeated the San Francisco 49ers 20-17 on January 22, 2012. This let them go to the Super Bowl. It was largely because of their ability to hold the ball. Including overtime, the Giants had the ball for 39:36, or 39 minutes and 36 seconds. The 49ers had it for 28:18.

The Giants wound up with 90 plays. The 49ers had 57 plays. The Giants led in first downs, 20-15. That helped them keep possession. They also did not lose possession through turnovers. The 49ers fumbled the ball twice.

The Giants had the ball for at least nine plays each of the first three times they had the ball. Those drives lasted 4:38, 4:58, and 4:16.

The 49ers had the ball longer than four minutes in only one drive during the game. They held the ball for just 0:29, 0:19, and 1:36 on their last three chances.

How much longer did the Giants hold the ball in their first three possessions than the 49ers did in their last three? For each team, add the minutes and seconds. Using the totals, subtract the times to find the answer.

Start with seconds for the Giants:
38 + 58 + 16 = 112 seconds or 1 minute 52 seconds
Then add the other minutes: 4 + 4 + 4 = 12 minutes
1 minute 52 seconds + 12 minutes = 13 minutes 52 seconds

Now add the seconds for the 49ers:
29 + 19 + 36 = 84 seconds or 1 minute 24 seconds
Add the other minute: 1 minute 24 seconds + 1 minute = 2 minutes 24 seconds

To find the difference, subtract the 49ers' minutes from the Giants' minutes.
13 minutes 52 seconds - 2 minutes 24 seconds = 11 minutes 28 seconds
The Giants' first three possessions were 11:28 longer than the 49ers' last three.

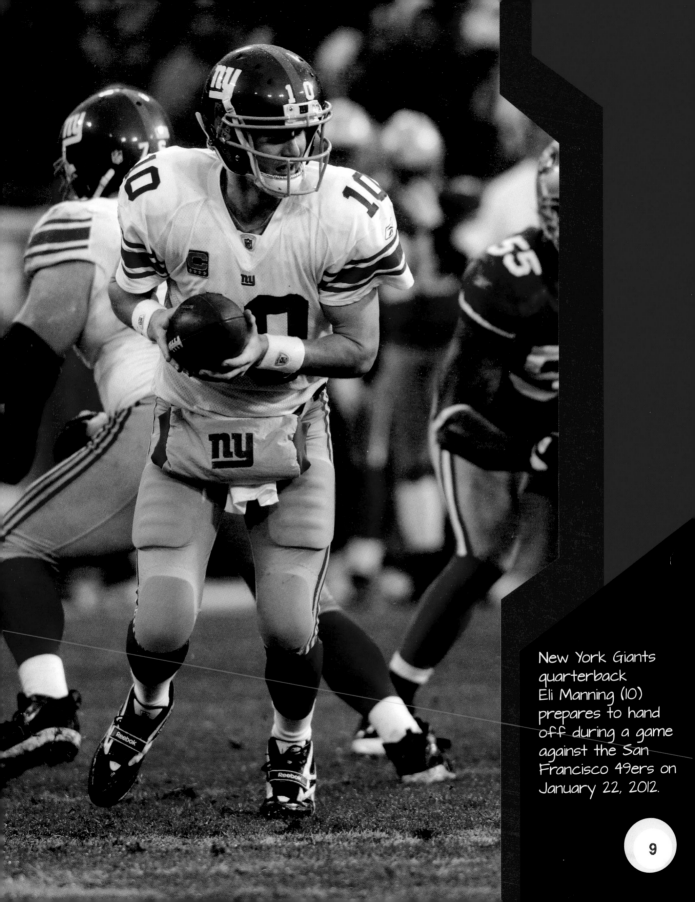

New York Giants quarterback Eli Manning (10) prepares to hand off during a game against the San Francisco 49ers on January 22, 2012.

New York Giants wide receiver Victor Cruz makes a catch during a game against the New York Jets on December 24, 2011.

Scoring Points

Victor Cruz of the New York Giants ran a precise pattern in the 2011 Christmas Eve game against the New York Jets. Cruz ran 10 yards down field and turned. He then pulled in a pass from Eli Manning. Cruz had enough yards for a first down, but he kept running. Then he outran the last Jet. He finished the 99-yard play. It was the longest possible play from the **line of scrimmage**. In one long play, the Giants made a touchdown. They picked up 6 points. They erased a 7–3 lead by the Jets.

Not every scoring play is so dramatic. Teams rarely cover 99 yards in one shot. And, they do not always get 6 points at a time.

Different scoring plays have different values.
- touchdown = 6 points
- field goal = 3 points
- safety = 2 points
- conversion = 1 or 2 points

The length of a touchdown is measured in yards from where the play started. A touchdown starting from the 50-yard line is a 50-yard play.

The length of a field goal is measured differently. Yards are counted from the goal post above the back of the end zone to where the ball is kicked. The ball is typically kicked from 7 yards behind where the play started.

If a team is planning to kick a field goal and the play is starting on the 15-yard line, how far will the kicker need to kick the ball?

Add 15 to the depth of the end zone (10). Also add the number of yards behind the line (7).
15 + 10 + 7 = 32 yards

The distance of the field goal is 32 yards.

Bloomsburg kicker Daniel Fisher (97) kicks an extra point in a game against Kutztown on November 6, 2010.

Conversions

Tim Tebow led the Denver Broncos to two touchdowns in the final minutes of an October 2011 game against the Miami Dolphins. After the second touchdown, the Broncos trailed 15–13. There were 25 seconds left.

Teams can go for one or two extra points after a touchdown. National Football League (NFL) coaches almost always choose to kick for one point. This game was different. It was one of the times a team tried a **two-point conversion**. That is to run or pass the ball from the 2-yard line for 2 points.

The Broncos needed 2 points to tie. That would force overtime. Tebow ran up the middle into the end zone and got the 2 points. Denver won in overtime 18–15 on a field goal.

There is a reason NFL coaches usually pick the kick for one extra point. In the 2011 regular season, NFL kickers made 1,200 out of 1,207 attempts. They were successful 99.4 percent of the time. Two-point conversions are less successful.

To find **percentages**, divide the number of successful attempts by the total attempts. Then multiply the number by 100. Percent means a number out of 100. All kinds of important statistics are measured in percentages.

NFL teams made 23 out of 52 attempts on two-point conversions in 2011.

$$23 \div 52 = 0.442$$
$$0.442 \times 100 = 44.2 \text{ percent}$$

The teams made 44.2 percent of their two-point conversions.

Teams kicking every time can expect to score 99 or 100 extra points for every 100 touchdowns. Teams that went for two-point conversions would expect about 88.4 extra points for every 100 touchdowns.

$$44.2 \text{ (percent)} \times 2 \text{ (points)} = 88.4 \text{ extra points}$$

THE PLAYERS

Big, Fast Guys

Baltimore Ravens quarterback Joe Flacco knows he is protected. The left offensive tackle is responsible for keeping pass rushers from getting the quarterback from behind. Baltimore's left tackle in 2011 was Bryant McKinnie.

Offensive linemen are often the biggest men on a football team. But few are bigger than McKinnie. He weighs 360 pounds and is 6 feet 8 inches tall. He has played ten seasons in the NFL.

The size and speed of players tends to vary by the positions they play. The off-season roster of the Chicago Bears shows average heights and weights of players as of May 2012. An average is one number that shows what is typical for a group of numbers.

To find an average, you first add up all the numbers in a group. Then you divide the total by the number of items in a group.

AVERAGE HEIGHTS AND WEIGHTS BY POSITION

POSITION GROUP	NUMBER OF PLAYERS	AVERAGE HEIGHT	AVERAGE WEIGHT
Quarterbacks	5	6 feet 4 inches	224 pounds
Running Backs	7	6 feet	224 pounds
Receivers	19	6 feet 2 inches	222 pounds
Offensive Linemen	16	6 feet 5 ½ inches	315 pounds
Defensive Linemen	11	6 feet 3 inches	293 pounds
Linebackers	14	6 feet 2 inches	238 pounds
Defensive Backs	16	5 feet 11 ½ inches	199 pounds
Kicking Specialists	4	6 feet ½ inch	194 pounds

University of Delaware offensive linemen Kevin Uhll (74) and Will Nagle (55) fire out of their stances to make blocks in a game against Maine on October 9, 2010.

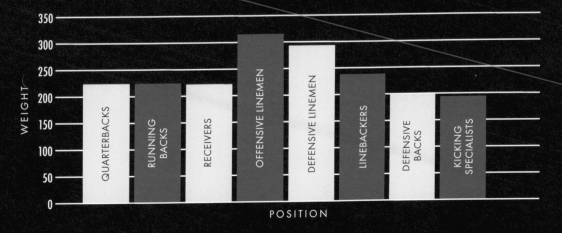

AVERAGE WEIGHTS BY POSITION

WEIGHT

350
300
250
200
150
100
50
0

QUARTERBACKS
RUNNING BACKS
RECEIVERS
OFFENSIVE LINEMEN
DEFENSIVE LINEMEN
LINEBACKERS
DEFENSIVE BACKS
KICKING SPECIALISTS

POSITION

Comparing Statistics

Statistics are used to compare many things in football, such as running, passing, receiving, and scoring. Passers are ranked by a ratings formula. Rushers are ranked by yards. Scorers are ranked by points. Receivers are usually ranked by either catches or yards.

Average yards per catch and touchdowns also appear in a list of leaders.

The following list shows 11 top receivers from the 2011 NFL season. It is ranked according to average yards per catch.

PLAYER	TEAM	CATCHES	YARDS	AVERAGE	TOUCHDOWNS
Victor Cruz	New York Giants	82	1,536	18.7	9
Jordy Nelson	Green Bay Packers	68	1,263	18.6	15
Vincent Jackson	San Diego Chargers	60	1,106	18.4	9
Julio Jones	Atlanta Falcons	54	959	17.8	8
Larry Fitzgerald	Arizona Cardinals	80	1,411	17.6	8
Steve Smith	Carolina Panthers	79	1,394	17.6	7
Calvin Johnson	Detroit Lions	96	1,681	17.5	16
Rob Gronkowski	New England Patriots	90	1,327	14.7	17
Jimmy Graham	New Orleans Saints	99	1,310	13.2	11
Roddy White	Atlanta Falcons	100	1,296	13.0	8
Wes Welker	New England Patriots	122	1,569	12.9	9

Gronkowski had 17 touchdowns on 90 catches.
90 ÷ 17 = 5.29, which can be rounded to 5.3
He had one touchdown for every 5.3 catches.

Green Bay Packers wide receiver Jordy Nelson (87) carries the ball during a game against the Miami Dolphins on October 17, 2010.

Rating the Passers

There are many ways to compare passing numbers. Some quarterbacks complete a high percentage of their passes. Others get more yards per pass. Some throw more touchdowns. Others are good at avoiding **interceptions**.

The best quarterbacks do well in each category. Aaron Rodgers, Drew Brees, and Tom Brady did that in 2011. They ranked at the top of many categories.

Here are the statistics of the top five NFL passers in 2011:

NFL TOTALS

PLAYER	TEAM	INTERCEPTIONS	YARDS	TOUCHDOWNS
Aaron Rodgers	Green Bay Packers	6	4,643	45
Drew Brees	New Orleans Saints	4	5,476	46
Tom Brady	New England Patriots	2	5,235	39
Tony Romo	Dallas Cowboys	10	4,184	31
Matthew Stafford	Detroit Lions	16	5,038	41

Comparing touchdowns to interceptions helps us compare quarterbacks. It is not part of the NFL's passing rating. But it is a good way to compare the success of passers. It points out the best players who make touchdowns while avoiding interceptions.

The touchdown-to-interception ratios of these five quarterbacks are:

Rodgers is 45:6
Brees is 46:14
Brady is 39:12
Romo is 31:10
Stafford is 41:16

Find the ratios in terms of number of touchdowns for each interception. To do this, divide touchdowns by interceptions.

For Rodgers:
$45 \div 6 = 7.5$.
His ratio is 7.5:1.

The ratios, rounded to the first decimal, are:

PLAYER	TOUCHDOWN-INTERCEPTION RATIO
Rodgers	7.5:1
Brees	3.3:1
Brady	3.3:1
Romo	3.1:1
Stafford	2.6:1

New Orleans Saints quarterback Drew Brees plays against the Carolina Panthers on October 9, 2011.

THE TEAM

Filling the Roster

Only 11 players take the field at a time for each team. Many more players get involved, though. Football is a rough sport, so players need breaks. Players with special skills are used in certain situations.

On the pro and college levels, players typically are separated into **offense** and **defense**. Many of those same players also fill roles on special teams that handle kicking plays. There are usually specific players just for kicking.

NFL teams have 53 players for each game. The coaches and general manager set that roster for each game.

Teams want the best players available. They also want to make sure to have enough players for each position.

When the New York Giants won Super Bowl XLVI early in 2012, their roster included:

NUMBER OF PLAYERS	CATEGORY	SPECIFIC POSITIONS
9	Defensive Backs	Cornerbacks, safeties
9	Offensive Linemen	Centers, guards, tackles
9	Receivers	Tight ends, wide receivers
9	Defensive Linemen	Tackles, ends
8	Linebackers	
5	Running Backs	Halfbacks, fullbacks
2	Quarterbacks	
2	Kicking Specialists	Kickers, punters

Quarterbacks and kicking specialists each make up a small part of the team. This can be shown on a circle graph. A circle graph can be used to show parts of a whole. A circle can be divided to show parts per hundred, or percents. To find this percentage, divide the total number of quarterbacks or kicking specialists (2) by the total number of players on the team.

2 (kicking specialists) ÷ 53 (players on the team) = .038
.0038 x 100 = 3.8 percent
Quarterbacks and kicking specialists are each 3.8 percent of the team.

The New York Giants' defense gathers on the field during a game against the Atlanta Falcons on January 8, 2012.

Defensive Backs 17%
Defensive Linemen 17%
Receivers 17%
Offensive Linemen 17%

Linebackers 15.1%
Running Backs 9.4%
Quarterbacks 3.8%
Kicking Specialists 3.8%

Turnover Differential

Defenses can take possession of the ball in two ways. They can intercept passes or recover fumbles by the offense. These are called turnovers. Turnovers are an important part of football.

Teams are compared by how many times they take the ball away and give it up. Totals are expressed in positive and negative numbers. This number is the turnover differential.

A number line helps compare negative numbers. When two numbers each have a negative sign, the larger number actually has a lesser value: -6 is less than -2.

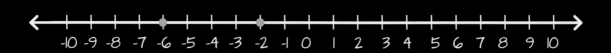

The double line graph shows the University of Toledo's takeaways and turnovers for each game in 2012. Toledo took the ball away more than it turned it over 7 times in 13 games. The takeaways add up to 30. The turnovers add up to 14.

30 - 14 = 16

The turnover differential is +16.

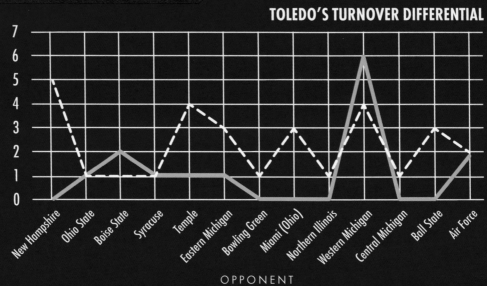

TOLEDO'S TURNOVER DIFFERENTIAL

- - - - Takeaways

——— Turnovers

OPPONENT

Bloomsburg defensive back Vince Browning (maroon) intercepts a pass intended for Kutztown receiver Josh Smith (white) on November 6, 2010.

Covering Space

The offense has wide receivers who can run the 40-yard dash in 4.4 seconds on each side of the field. The defense must prepare to defend their speed.

On a pass play that lasts 5 seconds before the ball reaches its target, how far down field could the wide receiver get?

Knowing a player's speed can help determine how much area a defensive player needs to cover.

The receiver runs 40 yards in 4.4 seconds. Divide 40 by 4.4 to find how many yards per second he runs.

40 ÷ 4.4 = 9.09 yards per second
Round that number to 9.1.
Multiply by 5 to find how many yards he runs in 5 seconds:
9.1 x 5 = 45.5 yards in 5 seconds

A defensive back needs to be able to get 45.5 yards from the line in 5 seconds to keep up with the speedy receiver.

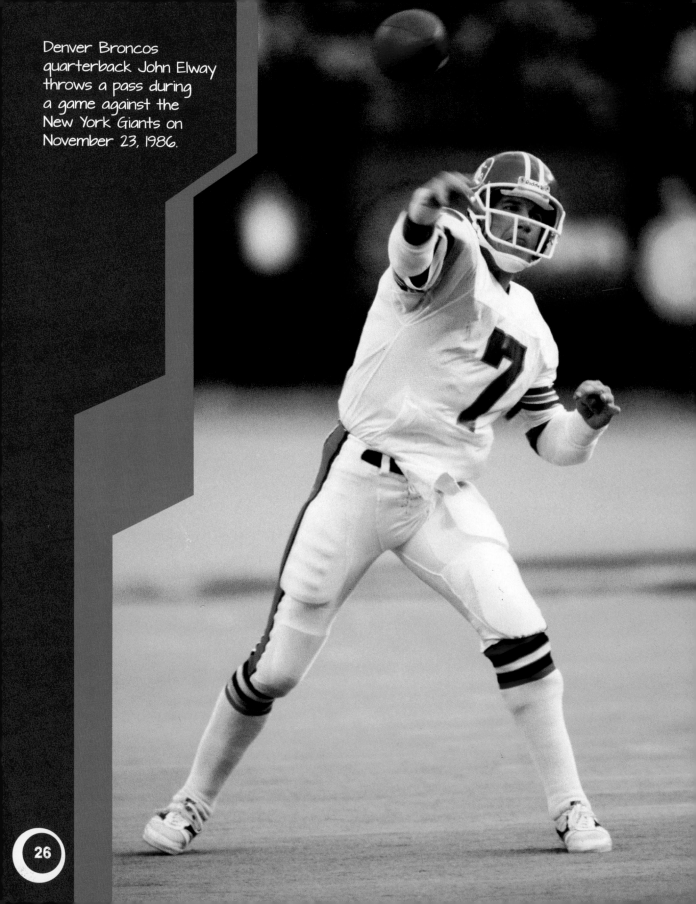

Denver Broncos quarterback John Elway throws a pass during a game against the New York Giants on November 23, 1986.

Two-Minute Drill

A typical NFL game features about 128 plays from the line of scrimmage. That is a little more than two plays per minute. That number goes up and down during the course of the game. At the end of each half, teams can get in more plays.

Teams practice the two-minute drill. In the drill, the offense hurries to get in as many plays as possible and move the ball down the field in two minutes.

One of the most famous cases of hurrying down the field came in the 1986 American Football Conference Championship game. John Elway led the Denver Broncos on what is now known simply as "The Drive." The Broncos got the ball back from Cleveland at its 2-yard line with 5:32 left. The Cleveland Browns led 20–13. The Broncos covered 98 yards and 15 plays in 4:55. They averaged better than three plays per minute.

The drive moved at a standard pace with seven plays in 3:33. By this point, it was clear. The drive was Denver's last chance to score and tie the game. The Broncos needed to get in as many plays as possible in the last 1:59.

Two completions, three incompletions, a sack, an out-of-bounds, and a 9-yard run by Elway put Denver deep in Cleveland territory. Elway threw a 5-yard touchdown pass to Mark Jackson with 37 seconds left. The extra point tied the game. The Broncos won 23–20 in overtime and went to the Super Bowl.

Denver ran the last eight plays in 1:22.

1:59 – 0:37 = 1:22

How does that compare to the typical two plays per minute? To find the answer, convert 1:22 to 82 seconds. There are 60 seconds in one minute.
60 + 22 = 82 seconds
Divide 82 by 8 to find how many seconds were in each play.
82 ÷ 8 = 10.25 seconds

This is approximately one play every ten seconds. This computes to six plays per minute.

GO FIGURE

1. LeSean McCoy gains 8, 17, and 6 yards on his first three carries. He loses 4 yards on his fourth attempt, then gains 6 on his fifth carry. After losing 2 yards on his sixth attempt, how many yards rushing does McCoy have?

2. David Akers lines up for a 45-yard field goal attempt. The ball is placed 7 yards behind the line of scrimmage for Akers to attempt his kick. On what yard line does the play start?

3. The following bar graph shows points allowed by the American Football Conference North teams during the 2011 regular season.

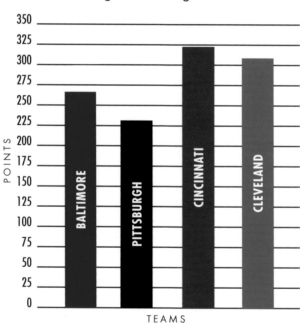

Which team allowed the fewest points?

4. Brett Favre passed 71,838 yards in his NFL career. To the nearest mile, how many miles worth of passes did he complete in his career? There are 1,760 yards in a mile.

San Francisco 49ers kicker David Akers (2) kicks a field goal during a game against the Philadelphia Eagles on October 2, 2011.

Answer Key

1. 8 + 17 + 6 + 6 = 37
   37 – 4 – 2 = **31 yards rushing**

2. 45 – 10 (yards in the end zone) = 35
   35 – 7 = **28-yard line**

3. Pittsburgh

4. 71,838 ÷ 1,760 = **41 miles**

defense (di-FENS): The defense on a team tries to stop the offense from scoring. On a football team, players are separated into offense and defense.

end zone (END ZONE): The end zone is the area at the end of a football field where the ball must be carried or passed to score points. Teams score touchdowns by crossing the goal line into the end zone.

field goal (FEELD GOHL): A field goal is a play in football in which the ball is kicked from the field through the goal posts, scoring three points. A field goal is worth three points.

first down (FURST DOUN): First down is the first of four downs that the offense has to try to advance the ball at least 10 yards. Getting a first down helps a team keep possession of the ball.

interceptions (in-tur-CEP-shunz): Interceptions happen when a defensive player catches a pass thrown by the other team. Some quarterbacks are good at avoiding interceptions.

line of scrimmage (LINE OV SKRIM-ij): The line of scrimmage is the imaginary line that separates teams at the beginning of play. Victor Cruz's 99-yard touchdown was the longest possible play from the line of scrimmage.

offense (uh-FENS): The offense on a team tries to score points. Defenses can intercept passes or recover fumbles by the offense.

percentages (pur-SEN-tij-iz): Percentages are numbers out of a hundred. All kinds of important statistics are measured in percentages.

statistic (stuh-TISS-tik): A statistic is a fact or piece of information expressed in a number or percentage. Total time of possession is a statistic used to compare teams in a game.

two-point conversion (TOO-POINT kuhn-VUR-shun): A two-point conversion is a scoring play that is made right after a touchdown, where the ball is carried or passed into the end zone from the 2-yard line. Two-point conversions are less successful than one-point kicks.

LEARN MORE

Books

Coffland, Jack, and David A. Coffland. *Football Math: Touchdown Activities and Projects for Grades 4–8*. Tucson, AZ: Good Year Books, 2005.

Mahaney, Ian F. *The Math of Football*. New York: Powerkids Press, 2012.

Marsico, Katie, and Cecilia Minden. *Football (Real World Math)*. Ann Arbor, MI: Cherry Lake, 2009.

Web Sites

Visit our Web site for links about football math:
childsworld.com/links

Note to Parents, Teachers, and Librarians: We routinely verify our Web links to make sure they are safe and active sites. So encourage your readers to check them out!

INDEX

Akers, David, 28
American Football Conference, 27, 28
area, 7
Arizona Cardinals, 16
Atlanta Falcons, 16
Baltimore Ravens, 14, 28
Belichick, Bill, 5
Brady, Tom, 5, 18, 19
Brees, Drew, 18, 19
Carolina Panthers, 16
Chicago Bears, 14
Cleveland Browns, 27, 28
conversions, 11, 13
Cruz, Victor, 11, 16
Dallas Cowboys, 18
defense, 20, 22, 24
Denver Broncos, 13, 27
Detroit Lions, 16, 18
Elway, John, 27
end zone, 6, 11, 13, 29
field size, 6–7
Fitzgerald, Larry, 16
Flacco, Joe, 14
Graham, Jimmy, 16
Green Bay Packers, 16, 18
Gronkowski, Rob, 16
Jackson, Mark, 27
Jackson, Vincent, 16
Johnson, Calvin, 16
Jones, Julio, 16

Manning, Eli, 11
McCoy, LeSean, 28
McKinnie, Bryant, 14
Miami Dolphins, 13
National Football League, 13, 14, 16, 18, 20, 27, 28
Nelson, Jordy, 16
New England Patriots, 5, 16, 18
New Orleans Saints, 16, 18
New York Giants, 8, 11, 16, 20
New York Jets, 11
offense, 20, 22, 24
percentage, 13, 18, 20
perimeter, 7
playing time, 8
ratios, 16, 18, 19
Rodgers, Aaron, 18, 19
Romo, Tony, 18, 19
roster, 14, 20–21
San Diego Chargers, 16
San Francisco 49ers, 8
scoring plays, 11
Smith, Steve, 16
Stafford, Matthew, 18, 19
Super Bowl, 8, 20, 27
Tebow, Tim, 13
two-minute drill, 27
turnover, 8, 22
Welker, Wes, 16
White, Roddy, 16